WOK COOKBOOK

WOK COOKING WITH DELICIOUS WOK RECIPES

By
BookSumo Press
Copyright © by Saxonberg Associates

Published by
BookSumo Press, a DBA of Saxonberg Associates
http://www.booksumo.com/

ABOUT THE AUTHOR.

BookSumo Press is a publisher of unique, easy, and healthy cookbooks.

Our cookbooks span all topics and all subjects. If you want a deep dive into the possibilities of cooking with any type of ingredient. Then BookSumo Press is your go to place for robust yet simple and delicious cookbooks and recipes. Whether you are looking for great tasting pressure cooker recipes or authentic ethic and cultural food. BookSumo Press has a delicious and easy cookbook for you.

With simple ingredients, and even simpler step-by-step instructions BookSumo cookbooks get everyone in the kitchen chefing delicious meals.

BookSumo is an independent publisher of books operating in the beautiful Garden State (NJ) and our team of chefs and kitchen experts are here to teach, eat, and be merry!

INTRODUCTION

Welcome to *The Effortless Chef Series*! Thank you for taking the time to purchase this cookbook.

Come take a journey into the delights of easy cooking. The point of this cookbook and all BookSumo Press cookbooks is to exemplify the effortless nature of cooking simply.

In this book we focus on Wok. You will find that even though the recipes are simple, the taste of the dishes are quite amazing.

So will you take an adventure in simple cooking? If the answer is yes please consult the table of contents to find the dishes you are most interested in.

Once you are ready, jump right in and start cooking.

— BookSumo Press

TABLE OF CONTENTS

About the Author...2

Introduction 3

Table of Contents 4

Any Issues? Contact Us 8

Legal Notes..9

Common Abbreviations 10

Chapter 1: Easy Wok Recipes 11

  Japanese Inspired Shrimp 11

  Ginger Tofu...14

  Chicken Tikka Masala 17

  Korma Vegetarian Edition 20

  Indian Style Curry Chicken................................23

  Indian Curried Red Lentils 26

  Makhani...29

  (Indian Butter Chicken II) 29

  Indian Style Curry Chickpeas 33

  Japanese Eggplants 36

Asian Corn Soup Cream Style 39

Tropical Hash 42

The Easiest Veggie Stir-Fry 45

Chicken Lo-Mein 47

Coconut Chicken 50

Sweet and Sour Ground Beef 53

BIBIMBAP 55

(VEGETARIAN APPROVED) 55

BULGOGI II 58

(KOREAN SPICY CHICKEN) 58

Friday Night Plum Steak 60

Sakura's Japanese Hot Dogs 63

Smoky Summer Green Beans 65

Classical Asian Green Beans 68

Teriyaki Green Beans 70

Jamaican Style Coconut Curry with Green Beans 72

Simple Mediterranean Escarole 75

Escarole Wok 77

Japanese Condensed Beef Steak Stir Fry 80

Japanese Chicken Drumsticks with Barbecued Beans and Hot Slaw 83

Chili Lime Seafood Soup 87

Fried Rice Cauliflower 90

Chinese Black Mushroom Fried Rice 93

Curried Apple and Raisins Fried Rice 97

Seafood Sampler Fried Rice 100

Hawaiian Fried Rice II 103

Ramen Noodle Beef Remix 106

Italian Ramen 109

Full Ramen Breakfast 112

Ramen Noodle Wok 115

Beef and Broccoli with Ramen Squares 118

Ramen Coleslaw 122

Ramen Lunch Box Salad 124

Romaine and Walnut Ramen Salad 127

Japanese Ramen 130

Southwest Ramen 133

Tangerine Chicken Stir Fry 136

Grilled Chicken Stir Fry Linguine 140

Basmati Chicken Stir Fry Spears............................142

Cashew Chicken Breasts Stir Fry 145

Roasted Nutty Chicken Stir Fry 148

Plum Peanut and Chicken Stir Fry.........................151

Beginners' Creamy Chicken Stir Fry 153

Italian Bell Chicken Stir Fry...................................155

Oriental Chili Chicken and Ramen Stir Fry 158

Corny Grilled Chicken Stir Fry...............................161

A Texas-Mexican Stir Fry.......................................164

THANKS FOR READING! JOIN THE CLUB AND KEEP ON
COOKING WITH 6 MORE COOKBOOKS.... 166

Come On..168

Let's Be Friends :)..168

ANY ISSUES? CONTACT US

If you find that something important to you is missing from this book please contact us at info@booksumo.com.

We will take your concerns into consideration when the 2nd edition of this book is published. And we will keep you updated!

— BookSumo Press

Legal Notes

COMMON ABBREVIATIONS

cup(s)	C.
tablespoon	tbsp
teaspoon	tsp
ounce	oz.
pound	lb

*All units used are standard American measurements

Chapter 1: Easy Wok Recipes

Japanese Inspired Shrimp

Ingredients

- 1 tbsp salt
- 2 C. cold water
- 1 lb shrimp, peeled and deveined
- 1/3 C. chicken broth
- 2 tsps rice wine
- 1 1/2 tsps soy sauce
- 1 1/2 tsps cornstarch
- 3/4 tsp sugar
- 1/8 tsp ground white pepper
- 1 tbsp vegetable oil
- 2 tbsps diced garlic
- 1 tsp diced fresh ginger root
- 2 tsps vegetable oil
- 6 oz. snow peas, strings removed
- 2 tbsps diced fresh chives
- 1/4 tsp salt

Directions

- Get bowl mix: water and salt, then shrimp. Let the shrimp sit in the water for 5 mins.
- Take out the shrimp and pat them dry with paper towels.
- Get a 2nd bowl, mix: pepper, broth, sugar, rice wine, cornstarch, and soy sauce. Place the mix to the side.
- Cook your shrimp in 1 tablespoon of olive oil with high heat in a wok. Stir fry this constantly so no burning occurs for about 1 min. Then add in 2 more tsps of oil, garlic, 1/4 tsp of salt, snow peas, and chives. Cook for another 1 min.
- Add in your broth and cornstarch and continue stir frying until everything is thick.
- Enjoy hot.

Amount per serving (4 total)

Timing Information:

Preparation	Cooking	Total Time
20 m	10 m	30 m

Nutritional Information:

Calories	207 kcal
Fat	7.8 g
Carbohydrates	7.8g
Protein	24.7 g
Cholesterol	173 mg
Sodium	2172 mg

* Percent Daily Values are based on a 2,000 calorie diet.

GINGER TOFU

Ingredients

- 1 lb firm tofu
- 1 C. fresh orange juice
- 1/4 C. rice vinegar
- 1/3 C. soy sauce
- 1/3 C. canola oil
- 4 tsps dark sesame oil
- 3 cloves garlic, diced
- 1 tbsp diced fresh ginger root
- 1/4 tsp red pepper flakes
- 1 green onions, cut into 1-inch strips
- 1/4 C. coarsely diced fresh cilantro
- 2 dried chipotle chili pepper (optional)

Directions

- Cut your tofu into 4 slices width-wide. Then cut out as many triangles as possible.
- Layer your tofu on a working surface and place some paper towel over them. Place on top of the paper towel something heavy like a wok and let the tofu drain for 45 mins.

- Get a bowl, mix: red pepper flakes, orange juice, ginger, vinegar, garlic, soy sauce, and oils.
- Set your oven to 350 degrees before doing anything else.
- Place your tofu into a casserole dish.
- Coat the tofu with the marinade. Top with some cilantro and green onions. Take the seeds from your chilies and any stems as well. Put the chilies in the tofu. Cover the casserole dish and let it sit in the fridge for 45 mins.
- Remove some of the liquid of the casserole dish so that only the bottom half of your tofu is covered.
- Cook in the oven for 50 mins.
- Enjoy with jasmine rice.

Amount per serving (4 total)

Timing Information:

Preparation	Cooking	Total Time
25 m		1 h 25 m

Nutritional Information:

Calories	419 kcal
Fat	33.6 g
Carbohydrates	14.6g
Protein	20 g
Cholesterol	0 mg
Sodium	1224 mg

* Percent Daily Values are based on a 2,000 calorie diet.

Chicken Tikka Masala

Ingredients
- 1 cup yogurt
- 1 tbsp lemon juice
- 2 tsps ground cumin
- 1 tsp ground cinnamon
- 2 tsps cayenne pepper
- 2 tsps freshly ground black pepper
- 1 tbsp minced fresh ginger
- 4 tsps salt, or to taste
- 3 boneless skinless chicken breasts, cut into bite-size pieces
- 4 long skewers
- 1 tbsp butter
- 1 clove garlic, minced
- 1 jalapeno pepper, finely chopped
- 2 tsps ground cumin
- 2 tsps paprika
- 3 tsps salt, or to taste
- 1 (8 ounce) can tomato sauce
- 1 cup heavy cream
- 1/4 cup chopped fresh cilantro

DIRECTIONS:

- Take lemon juice, yogurt, two tsps cumin, cayenne, cinnamon, ginger, black pepper, 4 tsps of salt and add into 1 mixing dish (possibly a big bowl).
- Add the chicken to the marinade, cover it, and place it in a refrigerator for 1 hour.
- Preheat a grill or frying pan to its highest heat.
- Add chicken to skewers and throw away the marinade.
- Add some butter or non stick spray to your grilling grate.
- Place the chicken on the grill and allow it to cook until its juices are clear. The approx. time is equal to about 5 minutes on each side.
- Take your butter and place it into a big wok or wok. The wok or wok should be placed over medium heat.
- For about 1 minute stir fry (sauté) some garlic and jalapeno.
- Take some paprika and cumin (approx. 2 tbsps each), and also three tsps of salt and add these ingredients to the garlic and jalapeno.
- Grab some cream and tomato sauce and place the two ingredients on low heat and continually stir the contents until they become thick. This process should take about 20 minutes.
- Combine everything with your grilled chicken and let everything cook for an additional ten minutes.
- Plate your contents and add some cilantro as a garnish.
- Enjoy.

Serving Size: 4 servings

Preparation	Cooking	Total Time
30 mins	50 mins	2 hrs 20 mins

Nutrition Information:

Calories	404 kcal
Carbohydrates	13.3 g
Cholesterol	143 mg
Fat	28.9 g
Fiber	2.5 g
Protein	24.6 g
Sodium	4499 mg

* Percent Daily Values are based on a 2,000 calorie diet

KORMA VEGETARIAN EDITION

Ingredients
- 1 1/2 tbsps vegetable oil
- 1 small onion, diced
- 1 tsp minced fresh ginger root
- 4 cloves garlic, minced
- 2 potatoes, cubed
- 4 carrots, cubed
- 1 fresh jalapeno pepper, seeded and sliced
- 3 tbsps ground unsalted cashews
- 1 (4 ounce) can tomato sauce
- 2 tsps salt
- 1 1/2 tbsps curry powder
- 1 cup frozen green peas
- 1/2 green bell pepper, chopped
- 1/2 red bell pepper, chopped
- 1 cup heavy cream
- 1 bunch fresh cilantro for garnish

DIRECTIONS:
- Grab your oil and add it to a wok or frying pan. Wok should be set over medium heat.
- Combine with oil, some onions, and let it cook until completely translucent. Next you should combine: garlic and ginger.

- Let the new mixture of cooked onions, garlic, and ginger, cook for approx. 1 minute.
- Grab some carrots, cashews, potatoes, and tomato sauce, and combine them all with some curry powder and salt for seasoning.
- Allow everything to cook for approx ten mins. taking care to stir consistently. Make sure that your potatoes are tender before moving to the next step.
- Take the following ingredients and stir them into your current mixture: peas, green and red bell peppers, and cream.
- Simmer everything for about 10 minutes on low heat.
- Plate your dish for serving.

Serving Size: 4 servings

Preparation	Cooking	Total Time
25 mins	30 mins	55 mins

Nutrition Information:

Calories	462 kcal
Carbohydrates	41.3 g
Cholesterol	82 mg
Fat	31 g
Fiber	8.4 g
Protein	8.6 g
Sodium	1434 mg

* Percent Daily Values are based on a 2,000 calorie diet.

INDIAN STYLE CURRY CHICKEN

Ingredients
- 3 tbsps olive oil
- 1 small onion, chopped
- 2 cloves garlic, minced
- 3 tbsps curry powder
- 1 tsp ground cinnamon
- 1 tsp paprika
- 1 bay leaf
- 1/2 tsp grated fresh ginger root
- 1/2 tsp white sugar
- salt to taste
- 2 skinless, boneless chicken breast halves - cut into bite-size pieces
- 1 tbsp tomato paste
- 1 cup plain yogurt
- 3/4 cup coconut milk
- 1/2 lemon, juiced
- 1/2 tsp cayenne pepper

DIRECTIONS:
- Grab a large wok or cooking dish. Place the pot over medium heat, let it get hot.
- Add some oil to the pot and stir fry some onions until they are slightly brown and translucent.

- Combine with the onions the following ingredients for seasoning: sugar, salt, ginger, 1 bay leaf, paprika, cinnamon, curry powder, and garlic.
- Take care to continually stir these ingredients together over the medium heat for at least two mins.
- Grab your yoghurt, tomato paste, coconut milk, and chicken pieces, add everything together, and let it cook until it begins to boil.
- Once the contents begin to bowl lower the heat on the stove and let everything simmer for about 20 to 25 mins.
- Add some lemon juice, and cayenne pepper and let it cook and simmer for an additional five mins.
- Plate and enjoy.

Serving Size: 4 to 6 servings

Preparation	Cooking	Total Time
20 mins	25 mins	45 mins

Nutrition Information:

Calories	313 kcal
Carbohydrates	14 g
Cholesterol	38 mg
Fat	21.7 g
Fiber	3.8 g
Protein	19.1 g
Sodium	268 mg

* Percent Daily Values are based on a 2,000 calorie diet.

INDIAN CURRIED RED LENTILS

Ingredients
- 2 cups red lentils
- 1 large onion, diced
- 1 tbsp vegetable oil
- 2 tbsps curry paste
- 1 tbsp curry powder
- 1 tsp ground turmeric
- 1 tsp ground cumin
- 1 tsp chili powder
- 1 tsp salt
- 1 tsp white sugar
- 1 tsp minced garlic
- 1 tsp minced fresh ginger
- 1 (14.25 ounce) can tomato puree

DIRECTIONS:
- Before you being, take your lentils, and wash them. Let water run over them until it runs clear without any traces of dirt or grime.
- Grab a nice sized pot and place in lentils and cover them with water and get it all boiling, cover the pot and take its heat level to medium.

- While your lentils are boiling you will have to add water continually to keep them covered. Cook the lentils until they are soft which will typically take about 15 to 20 mins.
- Once your lentils are tender you should drain the pot.
- Grab a large frying pan or wok and heat it up over medium heat. Add some oil and onions and fry them until they are caramelized (possibly 20 minutes of cooking time, take care to ensure your onions do not burn).
- Once the onions are caramelized combine the following ingredients for seasoning: turmeric, ginger, sugar, curry powder, cumin, chili powder, curry paste, and salt.
- Increase the heat of the wok and stir consistently until the ingredients begin to create a beautiful aroma, this will take about 1 to two minutes.
- Combine your tomato puree with the seasonings and remove everything from heat.
- Once removed from heat add your lentils and mix accordingly.
- Plate, serve, enjoy.

Serving Size: 8 servings

Preparation	Cooking	Total Time
10 mins	30 mins	40 mins

Nutrition Information:

Calories	192 kcal
Carbohydrates	32.5 g
Cholesterol	0 mg
Fat	2.6 g
Fiber	11.3 g
Protein	12.1 g
Sodium	572 mg

* Percent Daily Values are based on a 2,000 calorie diet.

MAKHANI

(INDIAN BUTTER CHICKEN II)

Ingredients
- 1 cup butter, divided
- 1 onion, minced
- 1 tbsp minced garlic
- 1 (15 ounce) can tomato sauce
- 3 cups heavy cream
- 2 tsps salt
- 1 tsp cayenne pepper
- 1 tsp garam masala
- 1 1/2 pounds skinless, boneless chicken breast, cut into bite-sized chunks
- 2 tbsps vegetable oil
- 2 tbsps tandoori masala

DIRECTIONS:
- The first step for this process is to preheat your oven to 375 degrees Fahrenheit or 190 degrees Celsius.
- Grab a wok and add 2 tbsps of butter. The wok should be heated with a medium level of heat.
- Make sure that your butter is fully melted and not burnt and begin to mix in some garlic and onions.

- Fry your garlic and onions for approx. 15 to 20 minutes until the onions have caramelized nicely.
- While you are frying your onions and garlic you should have another sauce pan with the remaining amount of butter present, heating over medium to high heat.
- Once the butter has melted fully in your second sauce pan begin to mix in the following ingredients: tomato sauce, heavy cream, cayenne pepper, salt, and some garam masala. Allow everything to cook until it has begun simmering.
- Once the second sauce pan is simmering lower the heat to a medium to low setting and cover the pan and let it simmer for 30 minutes. Make sure to stir the contents every few minutes.
- Once the onions have caramelized fully add them and the garlic to the second saucepan.
- Once everything has been combined and your sauce is simmering nicely make sure it is on low heat.
- Begin to mix chicken cubes with vegetable oil and add some tandoori masala in a separate bowl.
- Take some tbsps of sauce and add it to the chicken pieces to coat them evenly. Once the chicken has been coated with sauce, oil, and tandoori masala, spread each piece evenly over a baking dish.
- Place baking dish with seasoned chicken pieces into the preheated oven and cook for at least 12 minutes or longer. Just make sure your chicken is fully cooked and no longer pink in the middle.

- Once chicken is fully cooked, remove it from the oven, and combine it with the sauce and simmer for an additional 5 minutes.
- Plate and serve.

Servings: ≈4 servings

Preparation	Cooking	Total Time
15 mins	45 mins	1 hr

Nutrition Information:

Calories	880 kcal
Carbohydrates	12.8 g
Cholesterol	303 mg
Fat	82.3 g
Fiber	2.6 g
Protein	26.4 g
Sodium	1461 mg

* Percent Daily Values are based on a 2,000 calorie diet

INDIAN STYLE CURRY CHICKPEAS

Ingredients
- 2 tbsps vegetable oil
- 2 onions, minced
- 2 cloves garlic, minced
- 2 tsps fresh ginger root, finely chopped
- 6 whole cloves
- 2 (2 inch) sticks cinnamon, crushed
- 1 tsp ground cumin
- 1 tsp ground coriander
- salt
- 1 tsp cayenne pepper
- 1 tsp ground turmeric
- 2 (15 ounce) cans garbanzo beans
- 1 cup chopped fresh cilantro

DIRECTIONS:
- Grab a big wok or frying pan and heat it over a medium level of heat.
- Add some oil and onions to your pan and cook them down until they are tender.
- While your onions are frying add the following seasonings: turmeric, salt, cayenne, garlic, cinnamon, cumin, ginger, and coriander.

- Let your seasonings and onions continue to cook over the medium heat for about 1 to two minutes making sure to stir frequently.
- Grab some garbanzo beans and the associated garbanzo bean liquid and combine them with the seasoned onions.
- Mix and stir everything together and continue to cook until everything is well mixed and evenly heated.
- Combine some cilantro to the mix and before removing everything from the heating source.
- Plate, and enjoy. Garnish the food with fresh cilantro.

Serving Size: 8 servings

Preparation	Cooking	Total Time
10 mins	30 mins	40 mins

Nutrition Information:

Calories	135 kcal
Carbohydrates	20.5 g
Cholesterol	0 mg
Fat	4.5 g
Fiber	4.6 g
Protein	4.1 g
Sodium	289 mg

* Percent Daily Values are based on a 2,000 calorie diet.

Japanese Eggplants

Ingredients

- 2 tbsps vegetable oil
- 4 Japanese eggplants, cut into 1-inch cubes
- 2 tbsps vegetable oil
- 2 onions, thinly sliced
- 1 tbsp minced garlic
- 2 tbsps soy sauce
- 2 tbsps water
- 1 1/2 tbsps oyster sauce
- 1 tbsp chili garlic sauce
- 1 tsp white sugar
- ground black pepper to taste
- 1/2 tsp Asian (toasted) sesame oil

Directions

- Get a bowl, mix: black pepper, soy sauce, sugar, water, chili garlic sauce, and oyster sauce.
- Get 2 tbsps of oil very hot in a wok. Then stir fry your eggplants for 6 mins.
- Place the eggplants to the side.

- Add in 2 more tbsps of oil and then your onions and garlic for 1 min.
- Now pour in your soy sauce mix.
- Set the heat to low and pour the eggplants into the sauce and onions.
- Cook the eggplants with a light simmer and low heat until most of the liquid has evaporated (about 6 to 7 mins).
- Add some sesame oil and cook for 1 more min.
- Enjoy.

Amount per serving (6 total)

Timing Information:

Preparation	Cooking	Total Time
20 m	15 m	35 m

Nutritional Information:

Calories	212 kcal
Fat	10.3 g
Carbohydrates	29.9g
Protein	5 g
Cholesterol	0 mg
Sodium	445 mg

* Percent Daily Values are based on a 2,000 calorie diet.

ASIAN CORN SOUP CREAM STYLE

Ingredients

- 1/2 lb skinless, boneless chicken breast meat - finely diced
- 1 tbsp sherry
- 1/4 tsp salt
- 2 egg whites
- 1 (14.75 oz.) can cream-style corn
- 4 C. chicken broth
- 2 tsps soy sauce
- 1/4 C. water
- 2 tbsps cornstarch
- 4 slices crisp cooked bacon, crumbled

Directions

- Get a bowl, combine: chicken, egg whites, sherry, and salt.
- Combine in the cream corn and continue mixing everything until it's smooth.
- Now get the following boiling in a wok: soy sauce and chicken broth.
- Combine in the chicken mix and get everything boiling again.

- Now set the heat to low, and cook the soup for 5 mins while stirring.
- Combine some cornstarch and water then pour this mix into your boiling soup and keep stirring everything for 3 more mins. Then add in your bacon and serve.
- Enjoy.

Amount per serving: (6 total)

Timing Information:

Preparation	10 m
Cooking	30 m
Total Time	50 m

Nutritional Information:

Calories	157 kcal
Fat	3.3 g
Carbohydrates	16.2g
Protein	16 g
Cholesterol	26 mg
Sodium	1052 mg

* Percent Daily Values are based on a 2,000 calorie diet.

Tropical Hash

Ingredients

- 1/4 lb ground pork
- 1/4 lb shrimp - peeled, deveined and minced to a paste
- 1 egg white
- 2 tbsps diced water chestnuts
- 2 tbsps diced green onion
- 2 tbsps cornstarch
- 2 tsps soy sauce
- 1 tsp white sugar
- 1 tsp minced garlic
- 1 tsp oyster sauce
- 1/4 tsp salt
- 1/4 tsp ground black pepper
- 1/4 tsp sesame oil
- 1 (14 oz.) package round dumpling skins

Directions

- Get a bowl, combine: sesame oil, pork, pepper, shrimp, salt, egg white, oyster sauce, water chestnuts, garlic, green onions, sugar, cornstarch, and soy sauce.

- Add 1 tbsp of this mix to the middle of each of your wrappers.
- Coat the edges of the wrappers with some water then fold them up and crimp the top to form wontons.
- Steam the dumplings for 35 mins with a steamer basket place over some boiling water in a wok.
- Enjoy.

Amount per serving (25 total)

Timing Information:

Preparation	20 m
Cooking	30 m
Total Time	50 m

Nutritional Information:

Calories	64 kcal
Fat	1 g
Carbohydrates	10.1g
Protein	3.3 g
Cholesterol	11 mg
Sodium	151 mg

* Percent Daily Values are based on a 2,000 calorie diet.

THE EASIEST VEGGIE STIR-FRY

Ingredients

- 2 tbsps soy sauce
- 1 tbsp brown sugar
- 2 tsps garlic powder
- 2 tsps peanut butter
- 2 tsps olive oil
- 1 (16 ounce) package frozen mixed vegetables

Directions

- Get a bowl and combine the following ingredients: peanut butter, say sauce, garlic powder, and brown sugar.
- Grab a wok and heat your oil.
- Now begin to fry your veggies for 7 mins.
- Before serving season the veggies with some soy sauce.
- Enjoy

Servings: 6 servings

Timing Information:

Preparation	Cooking	Total Time
5 mins	5 mins	10 mins

Nutritional Information:

Calories	88 kcal
Carbohydrates	13.8 g
Cholesterol	0 mg
Fat	2.9 g
Fiber	3.3 g
Protein	3.5 g
Sodium	345 mg

* Percent Daily Values are based on a 2,000 calorie diet.

CHICKEN LO-MEIN

Ingredients

- 4 skinless, boneless chicken breast halves - cut into thin strips
- 5 tsps white sugar, divided
- 3 tbsps rice wine vinegar
- 1/2 C. soy sauce, divided
- 1 1/4 C. chicken broth
- 1 C. water
- 1 tbsp sesame oil
- 1/2 tsp ground black pepper
- 2 tbsps cornstarch
- 1 (12 oz.) package uncooked linguine pasta
- 2 tbsps vegetable oil, divided
- 2 tbsps diced fresh ginger root
- 1 tbsp diced garlic
- 1/2 lb fresh shiitake mushrooms, stemmed and sliced
- 6 green onions, sliced diagonally into 1/2 inch pieces

Directions

- Boil your pasta in water and salt for 7 to 10 mins until al dente. Drain the liquid and set aside.

- Get a bowl, mix: 1.4 C. soy sauce, 1.5 tsps sugar, and 1.5 tbsps vinegar. Add in your chicken, and cover the bowl with some plastic. Place everything in the fridge for 2 hrs.
- Get a 2nd bowl, mix: sesame oil, broth, black pepper, water and the remaining sugar.
- Get a 3rd bowl, mix: cornstarch, and some of the sesame mix.
- Combine both bowls (2nd and 3rd).
- Now begin to stir fry your chicken for 6 mins in veggie oil in a wok. Set aside. Then add in more veggie oil and stir fry your onions, ginger, mushrooms, and garlic for 1 min.
- Add the cornstarch mix, and cook for 3 to 5 mins until it becomes thick.
- Finally add the noodles to the mix and make sure all the noodles are coated evenly with sauce.
- Enjoy.

Amount per serving (4 total)

Timing Information:

Preparation	Cooking	Total Time
45 m	30 m	2 h 15 m

Nutritional Information:

Calories	603 kcal
Fat	14.9 g
Carbohydrates	78.9g
Protein	38.3 g
Cholesterol	62 mg
Sodium	2177 mg

* Percent Daily Values are based on a 2,000 calorie diet.

COCONUT CHICKEN

Ingredients

- 1 1/2 lbs skinless, boneless chicken breast halves - cut into 1 inch cubes
- 2 limes, zested and juiced
- 2 tbsps grated fresh ginger root
- 1 3/4 C. coconut milk
- 1/2 tsp white sugar
- 1 C. jasmine rice
- 1 tbsp sesame oil
- 1 tbsp honey
- 1/4 C. sweetened flaked coconut

Directions

- Get a bowl, combine: grated ginger, chicken breast, lime zest, and lime juice. Place a covering on the bowl and let the chicken marinate for 30 mins in the fridge.
- Get a saucepan and combine: sugar and milk. Get it lightly boiling then add in your jasmine rice. Set the high to low then place a lid on the pan and cook for 22 mins.

- Get a wok hot with sesame oil and then add in your chicken and the liquid. Cook for 5 mins stirring constantly with high heat.
- Add your honey and keep stirring so nothing burns.
- Shut off the heat and add in your coconut enjoy with rice.

Amount per serving (4 total)

Timing Information:

Preparation	Cooking	Total Time
15 m	25 m	1 h

Nutritional Information:

Calories	660 kcal
Fat	31.2 g
Carbohydrates	53g
Protein	43.8 g
Cholesterol	104 mg
Sodium	117 mg

* Percent Daily Values are based on a 2,000 calorie diet.

Sweet and Sour Ground Beef

Ingredients

- 1 lb ground beef
- 1/4 cup yellow mustard
- 1 tbsp balsamic vinegar
- 1 tbsp minced garlic
- 1 1/2 tsps soy sauce
- 1 1/2 tsps honey
- 1 1/2 tsps paprika
- 1/8 tsp ground black pepper

Directions

- Cook beef over medium heat in a wok for about seven minutes or until brown before adding mustard, paprika, balsamic vinegar, garlic, soy sauce, honey, and black pepper, and cooking all this for another three minutes.
- Serve.

Serving: 6

Timing Information:

Preparation	Cooking	Total Time
10 mins	5 mins	15 mins

Nutritional Information:

Calories	233 kcal
Carbohydrates	5.1 g
Cholesterol	71 mg
Fat	14.4 g
Fiber	0.9 g
Protein	20.2 g
Sodium	356 mg

* Percent Daily Values are based on a 2,000 calorie diet.

BIBIMBAP

(VEGETARIAN APPROVED)

Ingredients

- 2 tbsps sesame oil
- 1 C. carrot matchsticks
- 1 C. zucchini matchsticks
- 1/2 (14 oz.) can bean sprouts, drained
- 6 oz. canned bamboo shoots, drained
- 1 (4.5 oz.) can sliced mushrooms, drained
- 1/8 tsp salt to taste
- 2 C. cooked and cooled rice
- 1/3 C. sliced green onions
- 2 tbsps soy sauce
- 1/4 tsp ground black pepper
- 1 tbsp butter
- 3 eggs
- 3 tsps sweet red chili sauce, or to taste

Directions

- Stir fry your zucchini and carrots and in sesame oil for 7 mins then add in: mushrooms, bamboo, and sprouts.

- Stir fry the mix for 7 more mins then add in some salt and remove the veggies from the pan.
- Add in: black pepper, rice, soy sauce, and green onions. And get everything hot.
- Now in another pan fry your eggs in butter. When the yolks are somewhat runny but the egg whites are cooked place the eggs to the side. This should take about 3 mins of frying.
- Layer an egg on some rice.
- Add the veggies on top of the egg and some red chili sauce over everything.
- Enjoy.

Amount per serving (3 total)

Timing Information:

Preparation	Cooking	Total Time
30 m	20 m	50 m

Nutritional Information:

Calories	395 kcal
Fat	18.8 g
Carbohydrates	45g
Protein	13.6 g
Cholesterol	196 mg
Sodium	1086 mg

* Percent Daily Values are based on a 2,000 calorie diet.

Bulgogi II

(Korean Spicy Chicken)

Ingredients

- 1/4 C. diced onion
- 5 tbsps soy sauce
- 2 1/2 tbsps brown sugar
- 2 tbsps minced garlic
- 2 tbsps sesame oil
- 1 tbsp sesame seeds
- 1/2 tsp cayenne
- salt and ground black pepper to taste
- 1 lb skinless, boneless chicken breasts, cut into thin strips

Directions

- Get a bowl, combine: black pepper, onions, salt, brown sugar, soy sauce, cayenne, garlic, sesame seeds, and sesame oils.
- Add in your chicken to the mix and stir the mix before pouring everything in a wok.
- Stir fry the contents until your chicken is fully d1 for about 17 mins.
- Enjoy.

Amount per serving (4 total)

Timing Information:

Preparation	Cooking	Total Time
15 m	15 m	30 m

Nutritional Information:

Calories	269 kcal
Fat	11.6 g
Carbohydrates	13.2g
Protein	27.5 g
Cholesterol	69 mg
Sodium	1230 mg

* Percent Daily Values are based on a 2,000 calorie diet.

FRIDAY NIGHT PLUM STEAK

Ingredients

- 1.5 lbs rump steak
- 2/3 C. plum sauce
- 1 tbsp soy sauce
- 1 garlic clove, crushed
- 1 tsp fresh ginger, grated
- 1/2 tsp fresh red chili, chopped
- 2 tsp sugar
- 2 tsp dry sherry
- 2 tsp corn flour
- 2 tbsp oil
- 2 tsp corn flour, extra
- ½ C. water
- 1 small beef stock cube, crumbled

Directions

- Trim the steak and slice thinly.
- In a large bowl, mix together the steak slices, sauces, garlic, ginger, red chili, sugar, sherry and corn flour.
- Refrigerate, covered to marinate for at least 30 minutes or overnight.

- Remove the steak slices from the bowl and reserve the marinade.
- In a wok, heat a little oil and stir fry the steak slices in batches till browned.
- In a small bowl, dissolve the extra corn flour with water.
- In the wok, add all steak slices, reserved marinade, corn flour mixture and stock cube and bring to a boil, stirring continuously.
- Boil till the mixture thickens.
- Serve with the rice.

Servings per Recipe: 4

Timing Information:

Preparation	10 mins
Total Time	20 mins

Nutritional Information:

Calories	550.3
Fat	30.3g
Cholesterol	140.7mg
Sodium	778.6mg
Carbohydrates	26.6g
Protein	40.1g

* Percent Daily Values are based on a 2,000 calorie diet.

Sakura's Japanese Hot Dogs

INGREDIENTS

- 3 tbsp cooking oil
- 2 eggs, beaten
- 1/4 tsp salt
- 1/8 tsp freshly-ground pepper
- 3 C. cold cooked jasmine rice, fluffed
- 3/4 C. frozen peas and carrot, thawed
- 2 hot dogs, quartered lengthwise & sliced
- 1 1/2 tbsp soy sauce
- 4 green onions, thinly sliced

DIRECTIONS

- In a wok, heat 2 tbsp of the oil on high heat and cook the eggs, salt and pepper till lightly scrambled.
- Transfer the scrambled eggs into a plate and keep aside.
- Add the sliced hot dogs and stir fry for about 2 minutes.
- Add the remaining 1 tbsp of the oil, rice and stir fry for about 2 minutes.
- Add the peas and carrots and stir to combine well.
- Add the soy sauce, green onions and scrambled eggs and stir-fry for about 2-3 minutes.

Amount per serving: 4

Timing Information:

Preparation	15 mins
Total Time	25 mins

Nutritional Information:

Calories	349.7
Fat	19.6g
Cholesterol	104.9mg
Sodium	844.0mg
Carbohydrates	33.0g
Protein	10.1g

* Percent Daily Values are based on a 2,000 calorie diet.

SMOKY SUMMER GREEN BEANS

Ingredients

- 1 1/2 pounds green beans, trimmed, or more to taste
- 1 tbsp water, or as needed
- 1 tsp peanut oil
- 1 C. chopped onion
- 6 slices turkey bacon, or more to taste
- 3/4 C. brown sugar
- 3/4 C. apple cider vinegar
- 1/4 tsp liquid smoke flavoring
- 1/2 tsp ground black pepper

Directions

- Get a bowl for your green beans then add in water about 1 to 2 inches. Microwave the bean for 3 mins with a high of level of heat until the beans are soft but firm. Remove all the liquid.
- Add your peanut oil to a wok and begin to stir fry your onion for 9 mins. Place the onions in a 2nd bowl and remove all the oils from the wok.
- Add your bacon to wok and fry it until it completely done for 7 to 10 mins. Keep about 4 tbsps of oil in the pan, if

you do not have enough from the bacon then use peanut oil then place your fried bacon on paper towels to drain.

- Add the following to the wok: liquid smoke, onion, vinegar, and brown sugar. Stir fry everything for 5 mins then mix in your green beans and cook everything for 3 more mins.
- Place the entire dish into a baking dish and top with some black pepper.
- Enjoy.

Amount per serving 4

Timing Information:

Preparation	15 m
Cooking	15 m
Total Time	30 m

Nutritional Information:

Calories	270 kcal
Fat	7.5 g
Carbohydrates	43.3g
Protein	8.7 g
Cholesterol	15 mg
Sodium	340 mg

* Percent Daily Values are based on a 2,000 calorie diet.

CLASSICAL ASIAN GREEN BEANS

Ingredients

- 1 tbsp oil, peanut or sesame
- 2 cloves garlic, thinly sliced
- 1 pound fresh green beans, trimmed
- 1 tbsp white sugar
- 2 tbsps oyster sauce
- 2 tsps soy sauce

Directions

- Get your wok hot with peanut oil Then begin to stir fry your garlic for half a min then combine in the green beans and fry them for 6 mins. Add in the soy sauce, sugar, and oyster sauce. Keep frying for 3 more mins until the beans done.
- Enjoy.

Amount per serving 6

Timing Information:

Preparation	15 m
Cooking	10 m
Total Time	25 m

Nutritional Information:

Calories	55 kcal
Fat	2.3 g
Carbohydrates	8.1g
Protein	1.6 g
Cholesterol	0 mg
Sodium	141 mg

* Percent Daily Values are based on a 2,000 calorie diet.

TERIYAKI GREEN BEANS

Ingredients

- 1/2 C. peanut oil for frying
- 1 pound fresh green beans, trimmed and cut into 2-inch pieces
- 1 tbsp minced fresh ginger root
- 1 tbsp minced garlic
- 1 1/2 tsps teriyaki sauce
- 1/2 tsp white sugar
- 1 pinch black pepper

Directions

- Get your peanut oil hot in wok then stir fry your green beans in it for 3 mins with very hot oil. Place the bean in a bowl then keep about 3 tbsp of oil in the pot to stir fry your garlic and ginger in for 2 mins. Add the beans back in as well as the black pepper, sugar, and teriyaki.
- Cook everything for about 1 min more.
- Enjoy.

Amount per serving 4

Timing Information:

Preparation	15 m
Cooking	5 m
Total Time	20 m

Nutritional Information:

Calories	286 kcal
Fat	27.7 g
Carbohydrates	9.9g
Protein	2.4 g
Cholesterol	0 mg
Sodium	119 mg

* Percent Daily Values are based on a 2,000 calorie diet.

Jamaican Style Coconut Curry with Green Beans

Ingredients

- 1 tbsp vegetable oil
- 1 onion, sliced
- 1 serrano peppers, thinly sliced
- 1 clove garlic, crushed
- 5 fresh curry leaves
- 1 tbsp curry powder
- 1/2 tsp fenugreek seeds
- 1/4 tsp ground turmeric
- salt to taste
- 1 pound fresh green beans, trimmed
- 1/2 C. coconut milk
- 2 tbsps lime juice

Directions

- Get your oil hot in frying pan then begin to stir fry your curry leaves, onion, garlic, and serrano in the pot. Cook until the onions are nicely browned then combine in the salt, curry powder, turmeric, and fenugreek. Let the mix for about 4 more mins then combine in the green beans.

Toss everything then set the heat to low and the beans cook until the firm tender but firm. Add in the coconut milk and gently simmer the mix for 7 more mins.

- Shut the heat.
- Enjoy.

Amount per serving 6

Timing Information:

Preparation	20 m
Cooking	25 m
Total Time	45 m

Nutritional Information:

Calories	104 kcal
Fat	6.6 g
Carbohydrates	11.2g
Protein	2.6 g
Cholesterol	0 mg
Sodium	10 mg

* Percent Daily Values are based on a 2,000 calorie diet.

Simple Mediterranean Escarole

Ingredients

- 3 tbsp olive oil
- 2 medium heads escarole - rinsed, dried and chopped
- 1/2 C. lemon juice
- 2 tbsp capers
- 1 pinch salt
- 10 kalamata olives
- ground black pepper to taste

Directions

- In a wok, heat the oil on high heat and cook the escarole till just wilted.
- Stir in the lemon juice, capers, salt and olives and cook for about 15 seconds.
- Stir in the black pepper and serve immediately.

Amount per serving 3

Timing Information:

Preparation	10 m
Cooking	5 m
Total Time	15 m

Nutritional Information:

Calories	224 kcal
Fat	17.5 g
Carbohydrates	16.4g
Protein	4.8 g
Cholesterol	0 mg
Sodium	579 mg

* Percent Daily Values are based on a 2,000 calorie diet.

Escarole Wok

INGREDIENTS

- 2 lbs escarole
- 2 tbsp olive oil
- 2 tbsp vegetable oil
- 3 -4 cloves garlic, chopped
- 1/4 C. breadcrumbs
- red pepper flakes
- salt and pepper

Directions

- Chop the escarole roughly.
- In a large pan of boiling water, cook the escarole for about 2 minutes.
- Drain the escarole and rinse under cold water and then drain again.
- In a heavy wok, heat the oil on medium heat and sauté the garlic and red pepper flakes till the garlic is browned.
- Add the bread crumbs and cook till browned.
- Increase the heat to high.
- Stir in the escarole, salt and pepper and toss till heated completely.

- Transfer the escarole mixture in a serving bowl and top with any oil left in the pan.

Amount per serving: 4

Timing Information:

Preparation	10 mins
Total Time	20 mins

Nutritional Information:

Calories	188.3
Fat	14.3g
Cholesterol	0.0mg
Sodium	99.8mg
Carbohydrates	13.2g
Protein	3.8g

* Percent Daily Values are based on a 2,000 calorie diet.

JAPANESE CONDENSED BEEF STEAK STIR FRY

Ingredients

- 2 lb boneless beef sirloin or beef top round steaks (3/4" thick)
- 3 tbsp cornstarch
- 1 (10.5 oz) can Condensed Beef Broth
- 1/2 C. soy sauce
- 2 tbsp sugar
- 2 tbsp vegetable oil
- 4 C. sliced shiitake mushrooms
- 1 head Chinese cabbage (bok choy), thinly sliced
- 2 medium red peppers, cut into 2"-long strips
- 3 stalks celery, sliced
- 2 medium green onions, cut into 2" pieces
- Hot cooked regular long-grain white rice

Directions

- Cut the beef steak into thin strips.
- Get a mixing bowl: Whisk in it the cornstarch, broth, soy and sugar.

- Place a wok or pan over medium heat. Heat in it 1 tbsp of oil. Add half of the beef and cook it for 6 min. Drain it and place it aside. Repeat the process with the rest of the beef.
- Heat the remaining oil in the same pan. Cook in it the mushrooms, cabbage, peppers, celery and green onions for 6 to 8 min. Drain the veggies and place them aside.
- Add the broth mix to the same pan and cook them until they start boiling while stirring all the time. Keep boiling it until the mix becomes thick to make the sauce.
- Toss in back the cooked veggies and beef. Serve your stir fry warm with some white rice.
- Enjoy.

Amount per serving (8 total)

Timing Information:

Preparation	30 m
Cooking	15 m
Total Time	45 m

Nutritional Information:

Calories	290 kcal
Fat	7.6 g
Carbohydrates	26.4g
Protein	26.4 g
Cholesterol	39 mg
Sodium	1271 mg

* Percent Daily Values are based on a 2,000 calorie diet.

Japanese Chicken Drumsticks with Barbecued Beans and Hot Slaw

Ingredients

- 8 chicken drumsticks or 1 1/2-2 lbs chicken drumsticks
- 1 tbsp olive oil
- 1/4 C. ponzu sauce, lime sauce
- 1 tbsp ketchup
- 1/2 C. honey
- 1/2-1 garlic clove, minced
- salt and pepper
- 3/4 C. ketchup
- 1/2 C. pure maple syrup
- 1/2 tbsp liquid smoke flavoring
- 1/2 tsp dry mustard
- 1/4 tsp garlic powder
- salt and pepper
- 1 C. onion, chopped
- 2 C. canned black-eyed peas, drained and rinsed
- cooking spray
- 1/2 head cabbage, cored
- 1 medium carrot
- 1 tbsp olive oil
- 2 tbsp rice vinegar

- Ingredients
- 2 tbsp pure maple syrup
- 1 tbsp sriracha sauce
- 1 tbsp lime juice
- 1/2 tsp ground ginger
- salt

Directions

- To make the chicken drumsticks:
- Before you do anything preheat the oven to 375 F. Lay the chicken drumsticks in a greased casserole dish.
- Gct a small mixing bowl: Whisk in it the soy sauce, ketchup, honey, garlic, salt and pepper. Drizzle the mix all over the chicken drumsticks.
- Place the chicken pan in the oven and cook it for 30 min. Flip the chicken drumsticks and cook them for another 30 min.
- To make the barbecued beans:
- Place a heavy saucepan over medium heat: Stir in it the ketchup, pure maple syrup, smoke flavoring, mustard powder, garlic powder, salt and pepper. Cook them for 10 min.
- In the meantime, chop the onion and cook it in a greased pan for 6 min. Transfer the cooked onion with black eyed peas into the saucepan.
- Put on the lid and coo them until the bean becomes thick.

- Cut the carrot and cabbage into thin strips.
- To make the hot slaw:
- Grease a wok or a pan with a cooking spray. Cook in it the carrot and cabbage for 4 min.
- Get a small bowl: Whisk in it the olive oil, rice vinegar, pure maple syrup, Sriracha Hot Chili sauce, lime juice, ground ginger, salt and pepper to make the dressing.
- Drizzle the sauce all over the carrot and cabbage mix. Cook them for 3 min.
- Serve your chicken drumsticks warm with the barbecued beans and warm hot slaw.
- Enjoy.

Servings Per Recipe: 4

Timing Information:

Preparation	15 mins
Total Time	1 hr 15 mins

Nutritional Information:

Calories	746.4
Fat	20.5g
Cholesterol	118.2mg
Sodium	1063.7mg
Carbohydrates	109.2g
Protein	37.0g

* Percent Daily Values are based on a 2,000 calorie diet.

CHILI LIME SEAFOOD SOUP

Ingredients

- 1 tbsp vegetable oil
- 2 garlic cloves, finely chopped
- 2 finely chopped
- 1 tbsp chili sauce
- 1 tbsp tomato sauce
- 2 medium tomatoes cut into eighths
- 3 tbsp fish sauce
- 2 tbsp sugar
- 3 C. chicken stock
- 2 tbsp lime juice
- 8 oz fish fillets, cut into small pieces
- 4 oz scallops, sliced
- 4 oz raw shrimp, peeled and de-veined
- 12 mussels, scrubbed clean
- 2 tbsp dry white wine
- 1/4 tsp salt
- 1/4 tsp ground black pepper
- 2 leave cilantro, for garnishing

Directions

- Place a wok on medium heat. Heat the oil in it. Cook in it the shallot with garlic for 3 min.
- Stir in the chili sauce, tomato sauce, chopped tomato, fish sauce and sugar. Mix them well. Cook them for 4 min.
- Stir in the stock with lime juice. Cook them until it they start boiling. Stir in the wine with seafood. Cook them until they start boiling again.
- Put on the lid and cook them for 5 min. remove the mussels that stayed closed and didn't open. Adjust the seasoning of the soup. Serve it hot.
- Enjoy.

Amount per serving: 5

Timing Information:

Total Time	40 mins
Prep Time	20 mins
Cook Time	1hr

Nutritional Information:

Calories	251.2
Fat	6.4 g
Cholesterol	81.9 mg
Sodium	1436.6 mg
Carbohydrates	18 g
Protein	28.4 g

* Percent Daily Values are based on a 2,000 calorie diet.

FRIED RICE CAULIFLOWER

Ingredients

- 2 C. frozen peas
- 1/2 C. water
- 1/4 C. sesame oil, divided
- 4 C. cubed pork loin
- 6 green onions, sliced
- 1 large carrot, cubed
- 2 cloves garlic, minced
- 20 oz. shredded cauliflower
- 6 tbsp soy sauce
- 2 eggs, beaten

Directions

- In a pan, add the peas and water and bring to a boil.
- Reduce the heat to medium-low and cook for about 5 minutes.
- Drain the peas completely.
- In a wok, heat 2 tbsp of the sesame oil on medium-high heat and sear the pork for about 7-10 minutes.
- Transfer the pork into a plate.

- In the same wok, heat the remaining 2 tbsp of the sesame oil and sauté the green onions, carrot and garlic for about 5 minutes.
- Stir in the cauliflower and cook for about 4-5 minutes.
- Stir in the pork, peas and soy sauce and stir fry for about 3-5 minutes.
- Push the pork mixture to one side of the wok.
- Add the beaten eggs and cook for about 3-5 minutes, stirring continuously.
- Stir the cooked eggs into the pork mixture, breaking up any large chunks.
- Serve hot.

Amount per serving (6 total)

Timing Information:

Preparation	15 m
Cooking	30 m
Total Time	45 m

Nutritional Information:

Calories	366 kcal
Fat	19.2 g
Carbohydrates	15.8g
Protein	33.3 g
Cholesterol	132 mg
Sodium	1065 mg

* Percent Daily Values are based on a 2,000 calorie diet.

CHINESE BLACK MUSHROOM FRIED RICE

Ingredients

- 6 sticks dried bean curd
- 1 tbsp shredded black fungus
- 7 dried black mushrooms
- boiling water
- 3 1/4 C. water
- 2 C. basmati rice
- 1 tbsp butter or oil
- 4 eggs, beaten
- 3 tbsp vegetable oil
- 1 C. cubed carrots
- 1 C. chopped yellow onion
- 4 tbsp minced fresh ginger root
- 4 tbsp minced garlic
- 1/2 C. thinly sliced green onions
- 1 C. frozen peas
- 3 tbsp tamari
- 2 tbsp sesame oil
- fresh ground black pepper

Directions

- In a bowl of the boiling water, soak the the dried bean curd for about 20 minutes.
- In another bowl of the boiling water, soak the shredded black fungus and dried black mushrooms for about 20 minutes.
- In a pan, add 3 1/4 C. of the water and rice on high heat and bring to a boil.
- Reduce the heat to low and simmer, covered for about 5 minutes.
- Remove from the heat and keep aside, covered for about 20 minutes.
- In a non-stick wok, melt the butter on medium-high heat and scramble the eggs till creamy.
- Transfer the eggs into a bowl and chop into bits.
- In another bowl, mix together the carrot, onion, garlic and ginger.
- In a third bowl, mix together the green onions and frozen peas.
- Now drain all the water from the bean curd, fungus and mushrooms.
- Remove the tough bits from the bean and cut the remaining into quarter-inch rings.
- Slice the mushrooms.
- In a fourth bowl, mix together the bean curd and mushrooms.

- In a wok, heat 3 tbsp of the vegetable oil on high heat and cook the carrot, onion, garlic and ginger till tender, stirring occasionally.
- Stir in the bean curd, shredded fungus and mushrooms and stir fry for about 1 minute.
- Stir in the spring onion, frozen peas and rice.
- Stir in the eggs, tamari, sesame oil and a few twists of fresh black pepper and remove from the heat.

Amount per serving (6 total)

Timing Information:

Preparation	30 m
Cooking	30 m
Total Time	1 h

Nutritional Information:

Calories	539 kcal
Fat	19.8 g
Carbohydrates	71.7g
Protein	19.9 g
Cholesterol	129 mg
Sodium	613 mg

* Percent Daily Values are based on a 2,000 calorie diet.

CURRIED APPLE AND RAISINS FRIED RICE

Ingredients

- 6 oz. shrimp - peeled, veined, and cut into 1-inch pieces
- 1 pinch salt and ground black pepper
- 1 tsp cornstarch
- 1 tbsp vegetable oil
- 1 tsp minced garlic
- 1 egg, beaten
- 1 C. diced button mushrooms
- 3/4 C. frozen mixed vegetables
- 1 apple - peeled, cored, and diced
- 2 tbsp raisins
- 1 tsp curry powder
- 1 tbsp light soy sauce
- 2 C. overnight steamed white rice
- 1 green onion, diced

Directions

- In a bowl, mix together the shrimp, salt, pepper and cornstarch.
- In a wok, heat the oil on medium heat and cook the shrimp mixture for about 5 minutes.

- Transfer the shrimp mixture into a plate.
- In the same wok, add the garlic and sauté for about 1 minute.
- Add he egg and cook for about 3 minutes, stirring continuously.
- Stir in the mushrooms and cook for about 5 minutes.
- Stir in the mixed vegetables and cook for about 3-5 minutes.
- Stir in the apple, raisins and curry powder and cook for about 3 minutes.
- Stir in the rice, soy sauce, salt and pepper and cook for about 3-5 minutes.
- Stir in the shrimp mixture and green onion and cook for about 2-4 minutes.

Amount per serving (4 total)

Timing Information:

Preparation	30 m
Cooking	25 m
Total Time	55 m

Nutritional Information:

Calories	248 kcal
Fat	5.6 g
Carbohydrates	37.5g
Protein	12.7 g
Cholesterol	110 mg
Sodium	371 mg

* Percent Daily Values are based on a 2,000 calorie diet.

SEAFOOD SAMPLER FRIED RICE

Ingredients

- 2/3 C. uncooked long grain white rice
- 1 1/3 C. water
- 3 tbsp vegetable oil
- 2 medium onions, cut into wedges
- 3 cloves garlic, chopped
- 1/2 tbsp white sugar
- 2 tsp salt
- 1 egg, beaten
- 1/4 lb. cooked crab meat
- 3 green onions, chopped
- 1 tbsp chopped cilantro
- 1/2 cucumber, sliced
- 1 lime, sliced

Directions

- In a pan, add the rice and water and bring to a boil.
- Reduce the heat and simmer, covered for about 20 minutes.
- In a wok, heat the oil on medium heat and sauté the onions and garlic till tender.

- Stir in the rice, sugar and salt and cook for about 5 minutes.
- Stir in the egg and increase the heat to high.
- Stir in the crab meat, green onions and cilantro and cook for about 2-5 minutes.
- Serve with a garnishing of the cucumber and lime slices.

Amount per serving (4 total)

Timing Information:

Preparation	15 m
Cooking	40 m
Total Time	55 m

Nutritional Information:

Calories	304 kcal
Fat	12.2 g
Carbohydrates	37.4g
Protein	11.6 g
Cholesterol	68 mg
Sodium	1294 mg

* Percent Daily Values are based on a 2,000 calorie diet.

Hawaiian Fried Rice II

Ingredients

- 4 1/2 C. dry rice, cooked and cooled
- 6 -7 eggs, with a splash water, scrambled
- 1 (11 oz.) cans Spam lite, diced
- 1 yellow onion, diced
- 12 oz. frozen peas and carrots, thawed

SAUCE

- 1 C. aloha shoyu soy sauce
- 6 -7 tbsp for Kikkoman soy sauce
- 4 -5 garlic cloves, minced
- 2 tbsp oyster sauce
- 1 tsp sesame oil

Directions

- In a wok, heat 1/2 tbsp of the vegetable oil on medium-high heat and cook the eggs till scrambled.
- Transfer the scrambled eggs into a bowl.
- In the same wok, heat 1 tbsp of the oil on medium-high heat and sauté the onions and Spam till golden and starts to crisp.

- Meanwhile in a bowl, add all the sauce ingredients and stir till the sugar dissolves.
- Stir in the thawed peas, carrots and sauce mixture and bring to a boil on high heat.
- Cook till the mixture changes into a glaze.
- Slowly, add the cooled rice and eggs, breaking up any clumps of rice and cook till heated completely.
- Serve immediately.

Servings Per Recipe: 8

Timing Information:

Preparation	15 mins
Total Time	40 mins

Nutritional Information:

Calories	532.0
Fat	5.0g
Cholesterol	139.5mg
Sodium	2222.7mg
Carbohydrates	102.6g
Protein	17.5g

* Percent Daily Values are based on a 2,000 calorie diet.

Ramen Noodle Beef Remix

Ingredients

- 1 lb. top round steak, 3/4 inch thick, sliced across the grain, 1/4 inch thick x 1 inch long
- 1 tbsp peanut oil
- 1/2 tbsp sesame oil
- 1 inch fresh ginger, finely grated
- 2 cloves garlic, minced
- 1/4-1/2 tsp crushed red pepper flakes
- 3 C. beef stock
- 2 bunches scallions, 1/2 inch long, whites & light green
- 2 tbsp rice wine vinegar
- 2 (3 oz.) packets ramen noodles (discarded seasoning packet)
- 1/2 C. baby carrots, grated

Directions

- In a wok, heat 1/3 of both oils on medium-high heat and stir fry the garlic, ginger and red chilies for about 1 minute.
- Add 1/3 of the beef and stir fry for about 3 minutes.
- transfer the beef mixture into a bowl and keep aside, covered to keep warm.

- Repeat with the remaining beef.
- In the same wok, add the stock, vinegar and scallions and bring to a boil.
- Reduce the heat to low and simmer for about 10 minutes.
- Meanwhile in a pan of the boiling water, cook the ramen noodles for about 3 minutes.
- Divide the ramen noodles into 4 serving bowls and top with 1/4 of the beef.
- Divide the broth into bowls and top with 1/4 of the carrots.
- Serve immediately.

Servings Per Recipe: 4

Timing Information:

Preparation	20 mins
Total Time	45 mins

Nutritional Information:

Calories	467.9
Fat	21.3g
Cholesterol	78.2mg
Sodium	1630.6mg
Carbohydrates	35.4g
Protein	33.3g

* Percent Daily Values are based on a 2,000 calorie diet.

Italian Ramen

Ingredients

- 1/2 C. diced pancetta
- 1 tbsp olive oil
- 1 medium onion, chopped
- 1/4 tsp salt
- 1 (3 oz.) package ramen noodles, coarsely broken in package (flavor packet discarded)
- 1 (10 oz.) package frozen peas
- 3 C. low-chicken broth
- 1 tbsp butter
- 1/2 C. grated Parmesan cheese, plus additional for serving
- 1/4 tsp freshly ground black pepper

Directions

- In a 12-inch nonstick wok, heat the oil on medium heat and cook the pancetta for about 5 minutes, stirring occasionally.
- Stir in the onion and salt and cook for about 4 minutes, stirring continuously.
- Add the noodles and cook for about 1 minute, stirring continuously.
- Stir in the peas and broth and bring to a boil.

- Cook for about 3 minutes, stirring continuously.
- Remove from the heat and stir in the butter, Parmesan and pepper.
- Serve with a topping of the extra Parmesan.

Amount per serving (4 total)

Timing Information:

Preparation	5 m
Cooking	15 m
Total Time	20 m

Nutritional Information:

Calories	297 kcal
Fat	20.4 g
Carbohydrates	15.4g
Protein	13.2 g
Cholesterol	35 mg
Sodium	746 mg

* Percent Daily Values are based on a 2,000 calorie diet.

FULL RAMEN BREAKFAST

Ingredients

- 8 slices bacon
- 2 (3 oz.) packages ramen noodles, break each block into 4 pieces (flavor packets discarded)
- 1 1/2 tbsp vegetable oil, divided
- 1 C. shredded Cheddar cheese
- 1 tbsp butter
- 4 eggs

Directions

- Set your oven to 350 degrees F before doing anything else.
- Heat a 12-inch oven proof nonstick wok on medium heat and cook the bacon for about 8 minutes, stirring continuously.
- Transfer the bacon onto paper towels lined plate to drain.
- Remove wok from heat and discard the bacon grease, leaving 1 tbsp in the wok.
- In a pan of salted boiling water, cook the ramen noodles about 3 minutes, stirring occasionally.
- Drain the noodles in a colander and rinse under cold water.
- Heat the wok of bacon grease on medium-high heat.

- In the bottom of wok, place the noodles evenly and cook for about 3-6 minutes, pressing occasionally with a slotted spatula.
- Carefully, slide the ramen cake onto a large plate.
- Now, invert a second plate over top and flip cake over, cooked side upwards.
- In the same wok, heat 1 tbsp of the oil on medium-high heat.
- Carefully, slide ramen cake into wok and cook for about 3-5 minutes, pressing occasionally with a slotted spatula.
- Sprinkle with the cheese evenly and transfer the wok into oven.
- Cook in the oven for about 5-10 minutes.
- Remove from the oven and transfer ramen cake onto a cutting board.
- Carefully, cut into 4 wedges.
- With the paper towels, wipe out the wok.
- In the same wok, heat remaining 1/2 tbsp of the oil and butter on medium heat.
- Carefully, crack eggs into wok and cook for about 2-3 minutes.
- In each serving plate, place 1 ramen wedge, 1 fried egg and 2 bacon slices and serve.

Amount per serving (4 total)

Timing Information:

Preparation	5 m
Cooking	30 m
Total Time	35 m

Nutritional Information:

Calories	383 kcal
Fat	31.1 g
Carbohydrates	4.7g
Protein	20.7 g
Cholesterol	243 mg
Sodium	836 mg

* Percent Daily Values are based on a 2,000 calorie diet.

Ramen Noodle Wok

Ingredients

- 1 1/2 C. hot water
- 1 (3 oz.) package Oriental-flavor ramen noodle soup mix (seasoning packet reserved)
- 2 tsp vegetable oil, divided
- 8 oz. skinless, boneless chicken breast halves, cut into 2-inch strips
- 2 C. broccoli florets
- 1 C. sliced onion wedges
- 2 cloves garlic, minced
- 1 C. fresh bean sprouts
- 1/2 C. water
- 1/2 C. sliced water chestnuts
- 1 tsp soy sauce
- 1 tsp oyster sauce
- 1/4 tsp Chile-garlic sauce (such as Sriracha)
- 1 Roma tomato, cut into wedges

Directions

- in a small pan, add 1 1/2 C. of the water and bring to a boil.
- Add the ramen noodles and cook for about 2 minutes.

- Drain well and keep aside.
- In a large wok, heat 1 tsp of the oil on medium heat and cook the chicken for about 5 minutes.
- With a slotted spoon, transfer the chicken into a bowl, reserving drippings in the wok.
- With a piece of the foil, cover the bowl to keep chicken warm.
- In the same wok, add the broccoli, onion, and garlic on high heat and cook for about 3-5 minutes.
- Add the drained noodles, reserved seasoning packet, bean sprouts, water chestnuts, water, soy sauce, oyster sauce and Sriracha and stir fry for about 3-5 minutes.
- Stir in the tomato wedges and cook for about 2-3 minutes.

Amount per serving (2 total)

Timing Information:

Preparation	15 m
Cooking	15 m
Total Time	30 m

Nutritional Information:

Calories	438 kcal
Fat	14.1 g
Carbohydrates	47.6g
Protein	31.9 g
Cholesterol	65 mg
Sodium	1118 mg

* Percent Daily Values are based on a 2,000 calorie diet.

Beef and Broccoli with Ramen Squares

Ingredients

Ramen Noodle Cake:

- 2 (3 oz.) packages ramen noodles, breaking each block into 4 pieces (exclude seasoning packets)
- 2 tbsp vegetable oil, divided
- Sauce:
- 3/4 C. water
- 3 tbsp oyster sauce
- 1 tbsp low-soy sauce
- 1 tbsp cornstarch
- 1 tsp white sugar
- 1/2 tsp toasted sesame oil (optional)

Stir-Fry:

- 2 1/2 tbsp vegetable oil, divided
- 1/2 lb. broccoli florets
- 1/3 C. water
- 3 large cloves garlic, finely chopped
- 2 tbsp minced fresh ginger
- 1 lb. flat iron steak, thinly sliced across the grain
- 1/4 tsp salt

Directions

- Set your oven to 350 degrees F before doing anything else.
- In a pan of salted boiling water, cook the ramen noodles about 3 minutes, stirring occasionally.
- Drain the noodles in a colander and rinse under cold water.
- In a 12-inch nonstick wok, heat 1 tbsp of the oil on medium-high heat
- In the bottom of wok, place the noodles evenly and cook for about 3-6 minutes, pressing occasionally with a slotted spatula.
- Carefully, slide the ramen cake onto a large plate.
- Now, invert a second plate over top and flip cake over, cooked side upwards.
- In the same wok, heat 1 tbsp of the oil on medium-high heat.
- Carefully, slide ramen cake into wok and cook for about 3-5 minutes, pressing occasionally with a slotted spatula.
- Slide ramen cake onto a baking sheet and transfer in the oven to keep warm.
- Meanwhile in a bowl, add the sugar. cornstarch, oyster sauce, soy sauce, water and sesame oil and beat till well combined.
- In the same wok, heat 1 tbsp oil on medium-high heat and stir fry the broccoli for about 1 minute.

- Add the water and educe the heat to medium.
- Cook, covered for about 2-3 minutes.
- Transfer the broccoli into a bowl.
- With paper towels, wipe out the wok.
- In the same wok, heat 1 1/2 tbsp of the oil on medium-high heat and stir fry the garlic and ginger for about 10 seconds.
- Add the beef and salt and stir fry for about 2 minutes.
- Stir in the sauce mixture and bring to a boil, stirring continuously.
- Add the broccoli and cook for about 30 seconds, stirring continuously.
- Remove from the heat.
- Remove the ramen cakes from the oven and transfer onto a cutting board.
- Carefully, cut into 4 wedges.
- Divide ramen cake wedges onto serving plates.
- Top each ramen wedge with 1 C. of the beef-broccoli mixture and serve.

Amount per serving (4 total)

Timing Information:

Preparation	20 m
Cooking	20 m
Total Time	40 m

Nutritional Information:

Calories	377 kcal
Fat	29.3 g
Carbohydrates	12.8g
Protein	16.2 g
Cholesterol	52 mg
Sodium	563 mg

* Percent Daily Values are based on a 2,000 calorie diet.

Ramen Coleslaw

Ingredients

- 1/4 C. butter
- 1 C. sunflower kernels
- 1 (3 oz.) package ramen noodles, broken into pieces
- 1 head Napa cabbage, chopped
- 4 spring onions, diced
- 1/2 C. vinegar
- 1/2 C. vegetable oil
- 2 tbsp white sugar
- 2 tbsp soy sauce

Directions

- In a large wok, melt the butter on medium heat and stir fry the sunflower kernels and ramen noodles for about 3-5 minutes.
- Remove from the heat and transfer the noodles mixture into a large salad owl. Keep aside to cool.
- In the bowl of the noodles, add the Napa cabbage and spring onions.
- In another salad bowl, add the sugar, vinegar, vegetable oil, and soy sauce and beat till the sugar is dissolved.
- Place dressing over the salad and toss to coat.

Amount per serving (10 total)

Timing Information:

Preparation	15 m
Cooking	5 m
Total Time	20 m

Nutritional Information:

Calories	248 kcal
Fat	23.3 g
Carbohydrates	8.3g
Protein	4 g
Cholesterol	12 mg
Sodium	217 mg

* Percent Daily Values are based on a 2,000 calorie diet.

Ramen Lunch Box Salad

Ingredients

- 2 (3 oz.) packages any flavor ramen noodles, crushed
- 1/2 C. sunflower seeds
- 1 (16 oz.) package broccoli coleslaw mix
- 1/2 C. chopped fresh pineapple
- 1/2 C. chopped fresh cilantro (optional)
- 2 green onions (white and green parts), chopped
- Dressing:
- 1/2 C. white sugar
- 1/2 C. cider vinegar
- 1/2 C. olive oil
- 1/2 tsp sesame oil
- 2 pinches cayenne pepper (optional)
- 1/2 tsp freshly ground black pepper

Directions

- Heat a nonstick wok on medium-low heat and cook the ramen noodles and sunflower seeds for about 5-10 minutes, stirring occasionally.
- In a large bowl, mix together the broccoli coleslaw mix, pineapple, cilantro and green onions.

- In another bowl, add the ramen seasoning packets, sugar, olive oil, sesame oil, vinegar, cayenne pepper and black pepper and beat till smooth.
- Place the dressing over the slaw mixture and toss to coat.
- Stir in the toasted ramen noodles and sunflower seeds and serve immediately.

Amount per serving (8 total)

Timing Information:

Preparation	20 m
Cooking	5 m
Total Time	25 m

Nutritional Information:

Calories	340 kcal
Fat	21.9 g
Carbohydrates	33g
Protein	4.2 g
Cholesterol	0 mg
Sodium	446 mg

* Percent Daily Values are based on a 2,000 calorie diet.

Romaine and Walnut Ramen Salad

Ingredients

- 1/4 C. unsalted butter
- 1 (3 oz.) package uncooked ramen noodles, crushed
- 1 C. chopped walnuts
- 1 C. vegetable oil
- 1 C. white sugar
- 1/2 C. red wine vinegar
- 3 tsp soy sauce
- salt and freshly ground black pepper to taste
- 2 heads romaine lettuce, chopped
- 1 bunch broccoli, coarsely chopped
- 4 green onions, chopped

Directions

- In a large wok, melt the butter on medium heat and cook the ramen noodles and walnuts for about 5 minutes.
- Transfer the noodles mixture into a paper towels lined plate and keep aside to cool.
- In a small bowl, add the sugar, vegetable oil, soy sauce, vinegar, salt and pepper and beat till well combined.
- In a large serving bowl, mix together the noodle mixture, broccoli, lettuce and green onions.

- Place the dressing and toss to coat.

Amount per serving (8 total)

Timing Information:

Preparation	20 m
Cooking	5 m
Total Time	45 m

Nutritional Information:

Calories	557 kcal
Fat	43.3 g
Carbohydrates	41g
Protein	6.3 g
Cholesterol	15 mg
Sodium	295 mg

* Percent Daily Values are based on a 2,000 calorie diet.

JAPANESE RAMEN

Ingredients

Sauce:

- 1/2 C. hoisin sauce
- 1/2 C. water
- 1 tbsp cornstarch
- 1 tsp white sugar
- 1/2 tsp grated fresh ginger
- 1/4 tsp red pepper flakes
- kosher salt and freshly ground black pepper to taste
- 4 C. water
- 2 (3 oz.) packages ramen noodles (without flavor packet)

Stir-Fry:

- 2 tsp peanut oil
- 1 bunch asparagus, cut diagonally into 1-inch pieces
- 2 carrots, peeled and sliced diagonally
- 1/2 onion, sliced
- 3 cloves garlic, pressed
- 1 C. thinly sliced cooked chicken
- 2 C. sliced Napa cabbage
- 1 C. sliced mushrooms

Directions

- In a bowl, add the ginger, cornstarch, sugar, hoisin sauce, water, red pepper flakes, salt and black pepper and beat till well combined.
- In a large pan if the boiling water, cook the ramen noodles for about 3 minutes, stirring occasionally.
- Drain well and keep aside.
- In a nonstick wok, heat the peanut oil on medium-high heat and sauté the carrots, asparagus, onion and garlic for about 3-5 minutes.
- Stir in the chicken and cook for about 2 minutes.
- Add the mushrooms, cabbage and sauce and toss to coat.
- Reduce the heat to low and simmer, covered for about 3-5 minutes.
- Divide the noodles onto serving plates and top with the chicken mixture and serve.

Amount per serving (4 total)

Timing Information:

Preparation	35 m
Cooking	16 m
Total Time	51 m

Nutritional Information:

Calories	423 kcal
Fat	15.3 g
Carbohydrates	55.3g
Protein	18.2 g
Cholesterol	28 mg
Sodium	867 mg

* Percent Daily Values are based on a 2,000 calorie diet.

SOUTHWEST RAMEN

Ingredients

- 1/4 lb. ground beef
- 1 tsp taco seasoning mix
- 3 quarts water
- 3 (3 oz.) packages chicken-flavored ramen noodle soup, broken into bite-sized pieces
- 1 (14.5 oz.) can Mexican-style stewed tomatoes
- 1 C. water
- 1/2 C. sour cream
- 1/2 C. shredded Cheddar cheese

Directions

- Heat a wok and cook the beef for 5 to 7 minutes.
- Stir in the taco seasoning and remove from the heat. Keep aside.
- In a 5-quart pan, add 3 quarts of the water and bring to a boil.
- Add the ramen noodles and cook for about 3-5 minutes, stirring occasionally.
- Drain well and keep aside.
- In a bowl, add the tomatoes and with your hands, break into small pieces.

- In another bowl, dissolve 2 ramen noodles seasoning packets in 1 C. of the water.
- Add the seasoning mixture into the bowl of the tomatoes and mix well.
- In a pan, add the tomato mixture on medium heat.
- Stir in the ground beef and cook for about 3-5 minutes.
- Add the drained noodles and stir to combine.
- Stir in the remaining seasoning packet and remove from the heat.
- Immediately, add the sour cream and stir to combine.
- Serve with a topping of the Cheddar cheese.

Amount per serving (4 total)

Timing Information:

Preparation	10 m
Cooking	15 m
Total Time	25 m

Nutritional Information:

Calories	495 kcal
Fat	25.5 g
Carbohydrates	50.2g
Protein	16.3 g
Cholesterol	45 mg
Sodium	1573 mg

* Percent Daily Values are based on a 2,000 calorie diet.

Tangerine Chicken Stir Fry

Ingredients

- 1/2 onion, minced
- 1/2 C. water
- 1/2 C. tangerine juice
- 1/3 C. coconut aminos
- 1/3 C. coconut oil
- 4 green onions, sliced into rounds
- 2 cloves garlic, minced
- 1 (1 inch) piece fresh ginger, minced
- 1 tsp vinegar
- salt and ground black pepper to taste
- 2 lb boneless chicken breast, cut into cubes
- 1 C. string beans, trimmed, or to taste
- 1 C. chopped broccoli
- 1/4 C. ghee
- 1 (8 oz) package fresh mushrooms, sliced
- 1/2 onion, sliced
- 2 tbsp coconut oil
- 3 zucchini, spiralized
- 2 carrots, shredded

Directions

- Get a mixing bowl: Mix in it the onion, water, tangerine juice, coconut aminos, 1/3 C. coconut oil, green onions, garlic, ginger, vinegar, salt, and black pepper to make the marinade.
- Get a large mixing bowl: Toss in it half of the marinade with chicken.
- Fill a large pot with water and a pinch of salt. Cook it until it starts boiling. Cook in it the string beans and broccoli for 2 min.
- Remove them from the hot water and place them in a ice bath right away to cool down. Remove them from the water and place them aside.
- Place a large pan or wok over medium heat. Melt the ghee in it. Add the mushroom and cook it for 8 min. Drain it and add it to the broccoli and bean mix.
- Add the onion into the same wok and cook it for 8 min. Drain it and add it to the broccoli mix.
- Drain the chicken and reserve the marinade.
- Place a large wok over medium heat and grease it with some oil. Cook in it the chicken for 12 min while stirring them often.
- Transfer the cooked chicken to the broccoli mix.
- Place a large pan over medium heat. Heat 2 tbsp of coconut oil in it. Cook in it the carrot with zucchini for 4 min.

- Stir in the remaining half of the marinade with the reserved chicken marinade and the broccoli mix. Cook them for 8 min while stirring them often.
- Serve your stir fry chicken warm.
- Enjoy.

Amount per serving (6 total)

Timing Information:

Preparation	20 m
Cooking	35 m
Total Time	55 m

Nutritional Information:

Calories	467 kcal
Fat	29.2 g
Carbohydrates	17.1g
Protein	34.8 g
Cholesterol	108 mg
Sodium	552 mg

* Percent Daily Values are based on a 2,000 calorie diet.

GRILLED CHICKEN STIR FRY LINGUINE

Ingredients

- 1 (22 oz) package Tyson(R) Grilled and Ready(R) Fully Cooked Frozen Grilled Chicken Breast Strips
- 2 C. sliced fresh mushrooms
- 2 tbsp vegetable oil
- 2 C. frozen sweet pepper stir-fry
- 2/3 C. stir-fry sauce
- 1 lb linguine, prepared according to package directions

Directions

- Cook the chicken according to the instructions on the package.
- Place a large wok or pan over medium heat. Heat the oil in it. Add the mushroom and cook it for 5 min.
- Stir in the pepper and cook them for 3 min. Stir in the chicken with sauce and cook them for 4 min.
- Serve your stir fry hot with the linguine.
- Enjoy.

Amount per serving (6 total)

Timing Information:

Preparation	
Cooking	
Total Time	25 m

Nutritional Information:

Calories	559 kcal
Fat	12.7 g
Carbohydrates	66.3g
Protein	43.6 g
Cholesterol	88 mg
Sodium	335 mg

* Percent Daily Values are based on a 2,000 calorie diet.

BASMATI CHICKEN STIR FRY SPEARS

Ingredients

- 2 C. basmati rice
- 4 C. water
- 1 tbsp vegetable oil
- 1 red onion, cut into 1/2-inch slices
- 3 1/2 lb skinless, boneless chicken thighs, cut into 2-inch strips
- 1 tbsp minced fresh ginger root
- 6 cloves garlic, minced
- 3 C. crimini mushrooms, cut in half
- 12 fresh asparagus, trimmed and cut into 2-inch pieces
- 2 small red bell peppers, cut into 1/2-inch strips
- 1 tbsp fish sauce
- 1 egg
- 2 C. fresh basil leaves
- 1 C. fresh cilantro leaves, chopped
- 2 tbsp sesame seeds, for garnish
- tamari soy sauce to taste

Directions

- Cook the rice according to the directions on the package.

- Place a large wok or pan over medium heat. Heat the oil in it. Add the onion and cook it for 4 min.
- Stir in the chicken with ginger and garlic. Cook them for 8 min. Stir in the mushrooms, asparagus, bell peppers, and fish sauce. Cook them for 7 min.
- Stir in the basil and cook them for 1 min. Serve your stir fry right away with the white rice.
- Enjoy.

Amount per serving (4 total)

Timing Information:

Preparation	20 m
Cooking	50 m
Total Time	1 h 10 m

Nutritional Information:

Calories	1095 kcal
Fat	47.7 g
Carbohydrates	86.7g
Protein	77.8 g
Cholesterol	270 mg
Sodium	610 mg

* Percent Daily Values are based on a 2,000 calorie diet.

Cashew Chicken Breasts Stir Fry

Ingredients

- 2 (8 oz) skinless, boneless chicken breast halves, cut into thin strips
- 3 tbsp light soy sauce
- 1 (2 inch) piece fresh ginger, peeled and finely chopped
- 1 tbsp chopped fresh tarragon
- 1 tbsp brown sugar
- salt and ground black pepper to taste
- 1 tbsp vegetable oil
- 1 C. unsalted cashews
- 2 large carrots, peeled and cut into matchstick-size pieces
- 1 head cabbage, sliced
- 1 C. baby kale
- 1 tbsp sesame oil

Directions

- Get a large mixing bowl: Whisk in it the soy sauce, ginger, tarragon, and brown sugar. Add the chicken and stir them to coat.
- Place a piece of plastic on the bowl to cover it. Place it in the fridge for 3 h.

- Place a large pan or wok over medium heat. Heat the oil in it. Remove the chicken from the marinade it add it to the pan. Cook it for 6 min.
- Stir in the chicken marinade. Cook them until they start boiling for 4 min. Add the carrots with cashews. Cook them for 2 min.
- Divide the cabbage and kale on 4 serving plates then drizzle the sesame oil over them. Top them with the chicken stir fry. Serve them right away.
- Enjoy.

Amount per serving (4 total)

Timing Information:

Preparation	15 m
Cooking	10 m
Total Time	2 h 25 m

Nutritional Information:

Calories	501 kcal
Fat	24.6 g
Carbohydrates	38g
Protein	36.9 g
Cholesterol	66 mg
Sodium	783 mg

* Percent Daily Values are based on a 2,000 calorie diet.

Roasted Nutty Chicken Stir Fry

Ingredients

- 1 tbsp wok oil or peanut oil
- 1 lb skinless, boneless chicken breast halves - cut into bite-size pieces
- 1 medium red bell pepper, chopped
- 1 1/2 C. chicken broth
- 2 tsp soy sauce
- 1 tbsp sugar
- 1 clove garlic, minced
- 1/4 tsp ground cayenne pepper
- 1 (1 inch) piece fresh ginger root, peeled and chopped
- 1 tbsp cornstarch
- 1 bunch green onions, chopped
- 1 bunch cilantro, chopped
- 2 C. chopped dry roasted peanuts

Directions

- Place a large wok over medium heat. Heat the oil in it. Cook in it the chicken for 6 min. Add the bell pepper and cook them until they become tender.

- Get a small mixing bowl: Whisk in it the broth, soy sauce, sugar, garlic, cayenne pepper, ginger, and cornstarch. Stir it into the wok with green onion and cilantro.
- Cook them for 6 min until the sauce becomes thick. Fold in it the roasted peanuts. Serve your stir fry hot.
- Enjoy.

Amount per serving (6 total)

Timing Information:

Preparation	10 m
Cooking	25 m
Total Time	35 m

Nutritional Information:

Calories	437 kcal
Fat	29.1 g
Carbohydrates	18.8g
Protein	29.7 g
Cholesterol	46 mg
Sodium	155 mg

* Percent Daily Values are based on a 2,000 calorie diet.

Plum Peanut and Chicken Stir Fry

Ingredients

- 1 tbsp vegetable oil
- 1 green bell pepper, seeded and cubed
- 1 red bell pepper, seeded and cubed
- 1/4 C. sliced sweet onions
- 3/4 lb skinless, boneless chicken breast, cut into strips
- 2 1/2 tsp Caribbean jerk seasoning
- 1/2 C. plum sauce
- 1 tbsp soy sauce
- 1/4 C. chopped roasted peanuts

Directions

- Place a large pan or wok over medium heat. Heat the oil in it. Add the onion with pepper and cook them for 8 min. Drain the mix and place it aside.
- Stir in the chicken with jerk seasoning. Cook it for 6 min. Add the plum sauce with onion and pepper mix. Stir them well. Cook them for 6 min.
- Fold in the soy sauce with peanuts. Serve your stir fry warm.
- Enjoy.

Amount per serving (2 total)

Timing Information:

Preparation	15 m
Cooking	20 m
Total Time	35 m

Nutritional Information:

Calories	549 kcal
Fat	21.4 g
Carbohydrates	41g
Protein	44.3 g
Cholesterol	104 mg
Sodium	1621 mg

* Percent Daily Values are based on a 2,000 calorie diet.

Beginners' Creamy Chicken Stir Fry

Ingredients

- 1 lb skinless, boneless chicken breast halves, cut into bite size pieces
- 1/2 onion, chopped
- 1 green bell pepper, chopped
- 1/4 C. butter
- 1 tsp paprika
- 1 tsp garlic salt
- seasoning salt to taste
- 1 (10.75 oz) can condensed cream of mushroom soup
- 1/2 C. water

Directions

- Place a large pan or wok over low heat. Heat the butter in it until it melts. Add the chicken, onion and green bell pepper then cook them for 7 min.
- Add the paprika garlic salt and seasoned salt. Put on the lid and cook them for 17 min. Stir in the water with soup and bring them to a simmer.
- Cook the stir fry until it becomes thick. Serve it hot with some rice.
- Enjoy.

Amount per serving (4 total)

Timing Information:

Preparation	20 m
Cooking	40 m
Total Time	1 h 20 m

Nutritional Information:

Calories	305 kcal
Fat	17.5 g
Carbohydrates	8.3g
Protein	28.1 g
Cholesterol	96 mg
Sodium	1102 mg

* Percent Daily Values are based on a 2,000 calorie diet.

ITALIAN BELL CHICKEN STIR FRY

Ingredients

- 2 tbsp all-purpose flour
- 1 tsp garlic powder
- salt and pepper to taste
- 1 lb skinless, boneless chicken breast meat - cut into cubes
- 1 tsp vegetable oil
- 1 red bell pepper, sliced
- 1 small onion, chopped
- 1 C. sliced zucchini
- 1 C. sliced fresh mushrooms
- 1/4 C. chicken broth
- 1/4 C. Italian salad dressing

Directions

- Get a zip lock bag: Combine in it the flour, garlic powder, salt, and pepper with chicken dices. Seal the bag and toss them to coat.
- Place a large wok or pan over medium heat. Heat the oil in it. Cook in it the chicken dices for 7 min.
- Add the bell pepper, onion, zucchini, mushrooms, chicken broth, and Italian dressing. Put on the lid and cook them for 12 min. Serve your stir fry hot with rice or noodles.

- Enjoy.

Amount per serving (4 total)

Timing Information:

Preparation	15 m
Cooking	15 m
Total Time	30 m

Nutritional Information:

Calories	210 kcal
Fat	7.9 g
Carbohydrates	10.2g
Protein	24.2 g
Cholesterol	59 mg
Sodium	297 mg

* Percent Daily Values are based on a 2,000 calorie diet.

ORIENTAL CHILI CHICKEN AND RAMEN STIR FRY

Ingredients

- 1 1/2 C. hot water
- 1 (3 oz) package Oriental-flavor ramen noodle soup mix
- 2 tsp vegetable oil, divided
- 8 oz skinless, boneless chicken breast halves, cut into 2-inch strips
- 2 C. broccoli florets
- 1 C. sliced onion wedges
- 2 cloves garlic, minced
- 1 C. fresh bean sprouts
- 1/2 C. water
- 1/2 C. sliced water chestnuts
- 1 tsp soy sauce
- 1 tsp oyster sauce
- 1/4 tsp chile-garlic sauce (such as Sriracha(R)), or to taste
- 1 roma tomato, cut into wedges

Directions

- Pour 1 1/2 C. of water in a heavy saucepan. Cook in it the noodles for 3 min. Remove it from the water and place it aside.
- Place a large pan or wok over medium heat. Heat 1 tsp of oil in it. Add the chicken and cook it for 7 min. Drain the chicken and place it aside.
- Turn the heat to high. Add the broccoli, onion, and garlic. Cook them for 7 min.
- Stir in the ramen seasoning packet with noodles, bean sprouts, water, water chestnuts, soy sauce, oyster sauce, and chile-garlic sauce.
- Cook them for 6 min. Stir in the tomato and cook them for 4 min. Serve your stir fry hot.
- Enjoy.

Amount per serving (2 total)

Timing Information:

Preparation	15 m
Cooking	15 m
Total Time	30 m

Nutritional Information:

Calories	438 kcal
Fat	14.1 g
Carbohydrates	47.6g
Protein	31.9 g
Cholesterol	65 mg
Sodium	1118 mg

* Percent Daily Values are based on a 2,000 calorie diet.

Corny Grilled Chicken Stir Fry

Ingredients

- 3 skinless, boneless chicken breast halves - cut into strips
- 2 tbsp olive oil
- 1 onion, sliced
- 1 red bell pepper, seeded and cubed
- 1 yellow bell pepper, seeded and cubed
- 1 (15 oz) can baby corn, drained
- 1 tbsp white sugar
- 1 (16 oz) package frozen stir-fry vegetables
- 1 C. water
- 1 tbsp cornstarch
- 1 tbsp soy sauce

Directions

- Before you do anything preheat the grill and grease it.
- Cook the chicken strips in the grill for 8 min. Place them aside to lose heat completely. Cut them into dices.
- Place a large pan or wok over medium heat. Heat the oil in it. Cook in it the onion for 3 min.
- Stir in the red and yellow pepper, baby corn, and the stir-fry veggies. Turn the heat to high medium. Cook them for 17 min.

- Get a small mixing bowl: Whisk in it the cornstarch with water.
- Stir in the salt with chicken, sugar, soy sauce, and cornstarch mix. Cook them until the stir fry becomes thick. Serve it hot with some rice or noodles.
- Enjoy.

Amount per serving (4 total)

Timing Information:

Preparation	15 m
Cooking	20 m
Total Time	35 m

Nutritional Information:

Calories	313 kcal
Fat	9.6 g
Carbohydrates	29.1g
Protein	25 g
Cholesterol	52 mg
Sodium	915 mg

* Percent Daily Values are based on a 2,000 calorie diet.

A TEXAS-MEXICAN STIR FRY

Ingredients

- 1 tsp olive oil
- 1 green bell pepper, chopped
- 1 red bell pepper, chopped
- 2 tbsps all-purpose flour, or as needed
- 1 (1 ounce) packet taco seasoning mix
- 1 pound skinless, boneless chicken breast halves, diced
- 2 tsps olive oil
- 1 (15 ounce) can black beans, rinsed and drained
- 1/2 cup prepared salsa
- 1 cup shredded Cheddar cheese

Directions

- Get a wok, heat 1 tsp olive oil. Fry red and green peppers for 5 mins, remove them.
- Grab a bowl combine the following: taco seasoning and flour. Add your chicken. Coat the chicken.
- Get your wok. Heat 2 tsps of olive oil. Fry chicken for five mins, until cooked.
- Combine the peppers from earlier with the chicken and also add some salsa, and black beans.
- Stir fry, the chicken, the peppers, the beans, and salsa for 5 mins.
- Serve with cheddar cheese.
- Enjoy.

Servings: 4 servings

Timing Information:

Preparation	Cooking	Total Time
20 mins	15 mins	35 mins

Nutritional Information:

Calories	333 kcal
Carbohydrates	13.3 g
Cholesterol	94 mg
Fat	5.9 g
Fiber	1.7 g
Protein	32.1 g
Sodium	945 mg

* Percent Daily Values are based on a 2,000 calorie diet.

THANKS FOR READING! JOIN THE CLUB AND KEEP ON COOKING WITH 6 MORE COOKBOOKS....

http://bit.ly/1TdrStv

To grab the box sets simply follow the link mentioned above, or tap one of book covers.

This will take you to a page where you can simply enter your email address and a PDF version of the box sets will be emailed to you.

Hope you are ready for some serious cooking!

http://bit.ly/1TdrStv

COME ON...
LET'S BE FRIENDS :)

We adore our readers and love connecting with them socially.

Like BookSumo on Facebook and let's get social!

Facebook

And also check out the BookSumo Cooking Blog.

Food Lover Blog

Made in the USA
San Bernardino, CA
22 December 2018